I love you

to the moon

and back!

To: _____

From: _____

I love you to the moon and back because...

_____

_____

_____

_____

_____

I love you to the moon and back because...

_____

_____

_____

_____

_____

I love you to the moon and back because...

_____

_____

_____

_____

_____

I love you to the moon and back because...

_____

_____

_____

_____

_____

I love you to the moon and back because...

_____

_____

_____

_____

_____

I love you to the moon and back because...

_____

_____

_____

_____

_____

I love you to the moon and back because...

_____

_____

_____

_____

_____

I love you to the moon and back because...

_____

_____

_____

_____

_____

I love you to the moon and back because...

_____

_____

_____

_____

_____

I love you to the moon and back because...

_____

_____

_____

_____

_____

I love you to the moon and back because...

_____

_____

_____

_____

_____

I love you to the moon and back because...

_____

_____

_____

_____

_____

I love you to the moon and back because...

_____

_____

_____

_____

_____

I love you to the moon and back because...

_____

_____

_____

_____

_____

I love you to the moon and back because...

_____

_____

_____

_____

_____

I love you to the moon and back because...

_____

_____

_____

_____

_____

I love you to the moon and back because...

_____

_____

_____

_____

_____

I love you to the moon and back because...

_____

_____

_____

_____

_____

I love you to the moon and back because...

_____

_____

_____

_____

_____

I love you to the moon and back because...

_____

_____

_____

_____

_____

I love you to the moon and back because...

_____

_____

_____

_____

_____

I love you to the moon and back because...

_____

_____

_____

_____

_____

I love you to the moon and back because...

_____

_____

_____

_____

_____

I love you to the moon and back because...

_____

_____

_____

_____

_____

I love you to the moon and back because...

_____

_____

_____

_____

_____

I love you to the moon and back because...

_____

_____

_____

_____

_____

I love you to the moon and back because...

_____

_____

_____

_____

_____

I love you to the moon and back because...

_____

_____

_____

_____

_____

I love you to the moon and back because...

_____

_____

_____

_____

_____

I love you to the moon and back because...

_____

_____

_____

_____

_____

I love you to the moon and back because...

_____

_____

_____

_____

_____

I love you to the moon and back because...

_____

_____

_____

_____

_____

I love you to the moon and back because...

_____

_____

_____

_____

_____

I love you to the moon and back because...

_____

_____

_____

_____

_____

I love you to the moon and back because...

_____

_____

_____

_____

_____

I love you to the moon and back because...

_____

_____

_____

_____

_____

I love you to the moon and back because...

_____

_____

_____

_____

_____

I love you to the moon and back because...

_____

_____

_____

_____

_____

I love you to the moon and back because...

_____

_____

_____

_____

_____

I love you to the moon and back because...

_____

_____

_____

_____

_____

I love you to the moon and back because...

_____

_____

_____

_____

_____

I love you to the moon and back because...

_____

_____

_____

_____

_____

I love you to the moon and back because...

_____

_____

_____

_____

_____

I love you to the moon and back because...

_____

_____

_____

_____

_____

I love you to the moon and back because...

_____

_____

_____

_____

_____

I love you to the moon and back because...

_____

_____

_____

_____

_____

I love you to the moon and back because...

_____

_____

_____

_____

_____

I love you to the moon and back because...

_____

_____

_____

_____

_____

I love you to the moon and back because...

_____

_____

_____

_____

_____

I love you to the moon and back because...

_____

_____

_____

_____

_____

Made in the USA
Lexington, KY
21 September 2018